Spelling and vocabulary

Workbook

Ages 6–7

SCHOLASTIC ENGLISH SKILLS

Spelling and vocabulary

Scholastic Education, an imprint of Scholastic Ltd
Book End, Range Road, Witney, Oxfordshire, OX29 0YD
Registered office: Westfield Road, Southam,
Warwickshire CV47 0RA

www.scholastic.co.uk

© 2016, Scholastic Ltd

1 2 3 4 5 6 7 8 9   6 7 8 9 0 1 2 3 4 5

British Library Cataloguing-in-Publication Data
A catalogue record for this book is available from the British Library.

ISBN 978-1407-14218-0
Printed by Ashford Colour Press

Author
Sarah Snashall

Editorial
Rachel Morgan, Anna Hall, Jenny Wilcox, Red Door Media

Design
Claire Green, Neil Salt and Nicolle Thomas

Cover Design
Nicolle Thomas

Illustration
Adam Linley/Beehive Illustration

Cover Illustration
Eddie Rego

Contents

How to use this book

- *Scholastic English Skills Workbooks* help your child to practise and improve their skills in English.

- The content is divided into topics. Find out what your child is doing in school and dip into the practice activities as required.

- Keep the working time short and come back to an activity if your child finds it too difficult. Ask your child to note any areas of difficulty. Don't worry if your child does not 'get' a concept first time, as children learn at different rates and content is likely to be covered at different times throughout the school year.

- Check your child's answers at www.scholastic.co.uk/ses/spelling.

- Give lots of encouragement, complete the 'How did you do' for each activity and the progress chart as your child finishes each chapter.

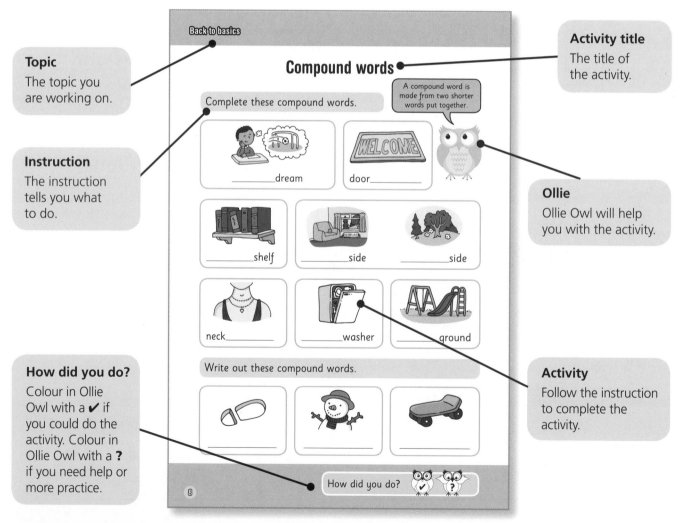

Topic
The topic you are working on.

Instruction
The instruction tells you what to do.

How did you do?
Colour in Ollie Owl with a ✔ if you could do the activity. Colour in Ollie Owl with a ? if you need help or more practice.

Activity title
The title of the activity.

Ollie
Ollie Owl will help you with the activity.

Activity
Follow the instruction to complete the activity.

If you need help, ask an adult!

Bear's sore paw

We can spell the /**or**/ sound in different ways:

cr**aw**l   f**or**k   sh**ore**   f**our**   s**au**ce

Read the words and listen to their endings.
Which word do they rhyme with?
Write them in the correct balloon.

source   score   drawn   pours   floors   born
horse   four   more   saws   yawn

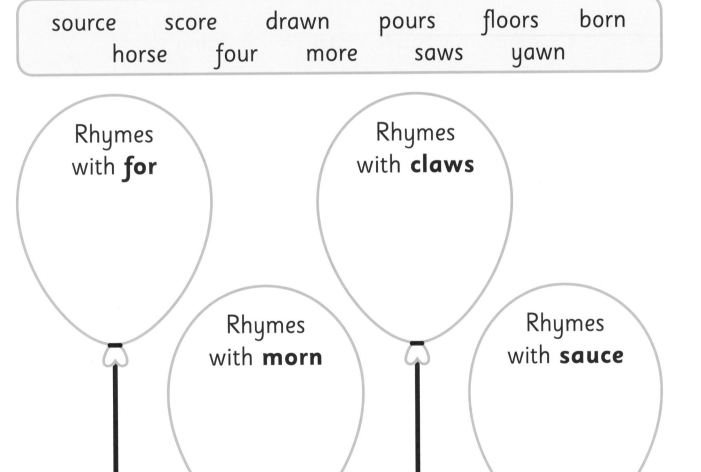

Rhymes
with **for**

Rhymes
with **claws**

Rhymes
with **morn**

Rhymes
with **sauce**

How did you do?

Spelling air, ear, are

Circle the word or phrase with the /**air**/ sound to complete these sentences.

1. Please **pair up** / **sort out** your socks.

2. Sit on the **chair** / **floor** and listen to me.

3. I am **sure** / **scared** that the wasp will sting me.

4. Please can you **share** / **stir** the pudding.

5. The brown **bunny** / **bear** has a soft tummy.

6. First, **tear up** / **turn over** the piece of paper.

7. Lizzie's **face** / **hair** is bright red.

8. All the **pears** / **peaches** are very juicy.

Circle the words with the /**air**/ sound in these sentences.

9. Be careful not to sit in the full glare of the sun.

10. Don't you dare go upstairs with those sweets.

11. We all stared when we saw what she was wearing.

How did you do?

Spelling with wh or w

Add **wh** or **w** to complete these words.

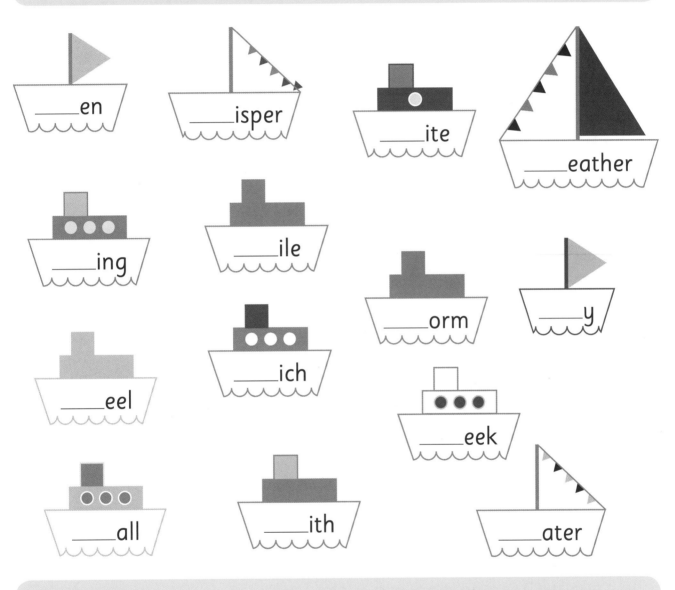

_____en

_____isper

_____ite

_____eather

_____ing

_____ile

_____orm

_____y

_____eel

_____ich

_____eek

_____all

_____ith

_____ater

Write **wh** or **w** to complete the words in the sentences.

1. Watch the television _____ile I'm cooking.

2. _____ere are my socks?

3. _____at have you done to your knee?

How did you do?

Compound words

Complete these compound words.

A compound word is made from two shorter words put together.

 _____dream

 door_____

 _____shelf

 _____side

 _____side

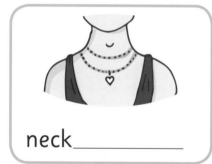 neck_____

 _____washer

 _____ground

Write out these compound words.

 _____

 _____

 _____

How did you do?

Adding s or es

Say the word aloud to check you have made the right choice.

Add **s** or **es** to complete these words.

apple_____   peach_____

catch_____   throw_____

cake_____   sandwich_____

search_____   find_____

teach_____   learn_____

push_____   pull_____

hit_____   miss_____

kiss_____   hug_____

How did you do?

Adding un

Add **un** to the beginning of these words.
Use the new words to complete the sentences.

_____loaded   _____lucky   _____sure   _____fair
_____packed   _____safe   _____tidy   _____dressed

1. The girls _____ their bags and then ran
    to the beach.

2. The old bridge looked too _____ to use.

3. Megan was _____ of the answer.

4. The happy boys had dirty clothes and _____ hair.

5. "That's _____!" said Maya. "She's already had
    a sweet!"

6. I was _____ at the school fair and didn't
    win anything.

7. Quickly, I got _____ and put on my
    swimming costume.

8. At the port, a crane _____ the containers
    from the ship.

How did you do?

Spelling the /j/ sound

Circle the word in each pair that is spelled correctly.

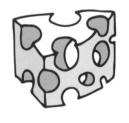

midge	mige
villadge	village
cottadge	cottage
fudge	fuge
messadge	message
splodge	sploge
strange	strandge
wedge	wege
ridge	rige
stadge	stage
badge	bage
sausadge	sausage

How did you do?

/j/ sound crossword

Use the words in the box to answer the clues and complete the crossword.

garage
bridge
hedge
judge
cage
charge
edge
huge

Across

2. To ask for money for something.

4. Very, very large.

5. The side of something.

6. The person who decides who wins a competition.

Down

1. A long thin platform for crossing rivers or roads.

2. A box made out of a metal mesh, for keeping animals in.

3. A place that fixes cars.

4. A trimmed bush at the edge of a garden or field.

How did you do?

Searching for the /j/ sound

Circle as many objects as you can find with the /**j**/ sound in this picture. Write down six of them.

The /**j**/ sound might be at the beginning, middle or end of the word.

How did you do?

Circling snakes

These words are all missing an /**s**/ sound.
Write **s** or **c** in the gaps to complete each word.

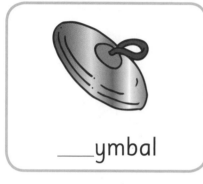

___ymbal

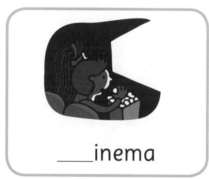

___inema

___ereal

___ailor

___ock

dan___e

___ity

___ircus

poli___e

___illy

___andwich

mi___e

How did you do?

I know a gnome

Write the word under each picture. The first one has been done for you.

Each word begins with the /**n**/ sound spelled **gn** or **kn**.

gnat

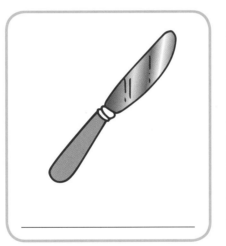

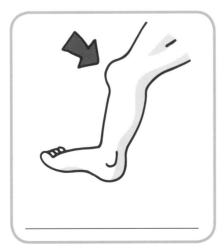

How did you do?

Writing the wrongs

Unscramble these letters to make real words.

Each word begins with **wr**.

gilgerw

_____

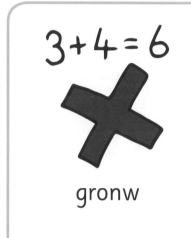

gronw

_____

newr

_____

triew

_____

awpr

_____

stirw

_____

Write the correct spelling of these words.

ritten _____

reck _____

rote _____

rinkle _____

How did you do?

Knocking knees

Add the missing letters to complete the sentences below.

All the missing letters are silent letters.

1. The ___night's ___nees ___nocked
    when he saw the dragon.

2. I don't ___now w___ere my ___nickers are.

3. The little ___ren sat on the ___nome's head.

4. Rhinos have ___rinkly ___nees.

5. I ___nocked on the door and ___neeled to look
    through the letter box.

6. I tied the ___not in the ___rong way.

7. It is ___rong to lick the butter off a ___nife.

8. I ___rapped up the scarf I had ___nitted for Granny.

How did you do?

Puzzle it out

Write the missing words in the gaps in these sentences.

Each missing word ends with **le**.

1. We sat and did a jigsaw p_____.

2. We put on the k_____ for a cup of tea.

3. Snow White took a bite out of the red a_____.

4. A b_____ landed on my nose in the bath.

5. I need a n_____ and thread to mend my shirt.

6. The sour milk tasted h_____.

How did you do?

Searching high and low

Find these **el** words in the word search and circle them.

model	hotel	travel	towel	parcel	kennel
camel	tunnel	squirrel	angel		

q	f	g	t	e	k	j	f	u	p	f
g	j	r	s	e	e	a	e	w	t	j
k	s	l	t	u	n	n	e	l	r	e
d	d	g	g	g	n	g	b	z	a	w
j	a	t	x	d	e	e	s	a	v	b
s	h	o	t	e	l	l	q	v	e	i
j	s	w	a	g	s	h	u	a	l	e
k	d	e	l	u	d	a	i	a	f	l
d	v	l	e	h	p	a	r	c	e	l
v	c	j	a	x	d	m	r	b	g	k
c	a	m	e	l	a	a	e	m	s	y
g	h	j	m	o	d	e	l	s	h	l

How did you do?

The royal poodle

Can you find 12 words ending in **al** in this story?
Circle the words and write them at the bottom of the sheet.

Every morning, Dominic Donut would pedal his bike across the capital to the animal hospital where he worked. On a normal morning the roads were clear, but one day, Dominic's way to work was blocked by a festival. It was total chaos and he could not get past. He tried to signal to several policemen but they were watching the princess's carriage go by. Just then the royal poodle jumped out of the carriage and ran underneath it. In general, Dominic was not a brave man, but he dashed under the carriage and scooped up the silly dog. The princess gave Dominic a medal and a lift to work.

How did you do?

A fine ending

Write the correct endings for the words below.

bott_____

hospit_____

All of these words end with the /ul/ sound. This ending can be spelled **al**, **el** or **le**.

eag_____

med_____

funn_____

ped_____

hand_____

ang_____

How did you do?

21

Beginnings and endings

Match up the parts of the words. Write the words at the bottom. Practise spelling the words.

pu	zil
ger	ssil
un	tril
pen	pil
Bra	til
pe	cil
fo	bil
nos	ril

How did you do?

It's a pleasure

The letters **su** and **si** make a buzzy /**zh**/ sound.

Circle the letters **su** or **si** in these words.

pleasure   decision   usual   measure

explosion   treasure   television   invasion

Underline the /**zh**/ words in these sentences.

1. We heard about an alien invasion on the television.

2. The pirates measured out the treasure with pleasure.

3. It is usual to first measure out the ingredients.

4. The policeman made a decision about the explosion.

Cover the top of the sheet. Finish these words.

explo_____

televi_____

trea_____

plea_____

How did you do?

23

Words ending with tion

Circle the part of each word that sounds like /**shun**/.

action   fractions   directions   information   station

competition   attention   nation   pollution

Use the words above to complete these sentences.

I have made a cake for the baking _____

at school.

I asked a lady the _____ to the train

_____ .

We read some _____ books about

_____ in rivers.

I paid extra _____ when our teacher

explained _____ .

Cover the top of the sheet. Complete these words.

sta_____   direc_____   informa_____

How did you do?

Last four letters

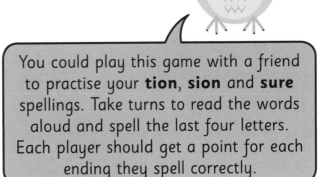

Throw a counter onto the grid below. Quickly cover the word that it lands on and write down the last four letters of the word on a separate piece of paper.

You could play this game with a friend to practise your **tion**, **sion** and **sure** spellings. Take turns to read the words aloud and spell the last four letters. Each player should get a point for each ending they spell correctly.

nation	direction	measure	division
occasion	unusual	usual	pollution
fraction	information	station	television
action	explosion	competition	pleasure
invasion	treasure	attention	decision

How did you do?

Fly, sky, fry

Circle the words that end with a **y**.

When we hear an /**igh**/ sound at the end of a word, it is often spelled with a **y**.

1. Apply sun cream in July by the sea.

2. Why is my sister so shy?

3. We are sly and spy on my brother.

4. Don't cry – there is a good supply of bacon to fry.

5. The birds fly up in the sky to dry their wings.

Write a sentence for each of these words.

sty _____

reply _____

Circle the words below that have an /**igh**/ sound that is spelled **y** in the middle.

My dad cycles to work.

Eek – there's a python in the tree.

How did you do?

Chimney, turkey, valley

These words all end in an /**ee**/ sound that is spelled **ey**.

> valley   chimney   turkey   jersey   alley
> honey   journey   monkey

Use the words above to answer the clues below

A sweet sticky treat made by bees. _____

A furry animal with a tail that swings from tree to tree in the jungle. _____

A large bird that does not fly, often eaten on Christmas Day. _____

On old-fashioned word for a jumper. _____

A low area between two hills. _____

A trip from one place to another. _____

A pathway between two fences. _____

A clay or concrete tube that lets smoke out of a building.

_____

How did you do?

Practising ey and y spellings

Sort these words into the cloud or the honey pot.

why   alley   my   honey   dry   turkey   fly   journey
July   monkey   by   valley   shy   sky

/ee/ spelt ey

/igh/ spelt y

How do these words end? Write **ey** or **y** to complete them.

1. cr_____

2. donk_____

3. k_____

4. fr_____

5. magnif_____

6. chimn_____

How did you do?

Mothers and brothers

Circle the letter **o** making an /**u**/ sound in each of these words.

other   another   mother   brother   nothing   Monday

month   oven   dozen   some   glove   love   above

honey   money   cover   monkey   dove

Use some of the words in the box to label this picture.
Draw lines from the words to the items in the picture.

How did you do?

Wall, call, ball

Read these words.

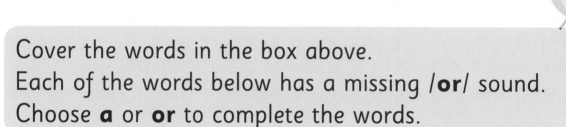

walk   ball   talk   walk   stalk   chalk

also   always   bald   ball   call   hall

fall   stall   all   tall   wall   small

Sometimes the /**or**/ sound is spelled with an **a** when it comes before **l** or **ll**.

Cover the words in the box above.
Each of the words below has a missing /**or**/ sound.
Choose **a** or **or** to complete the words.

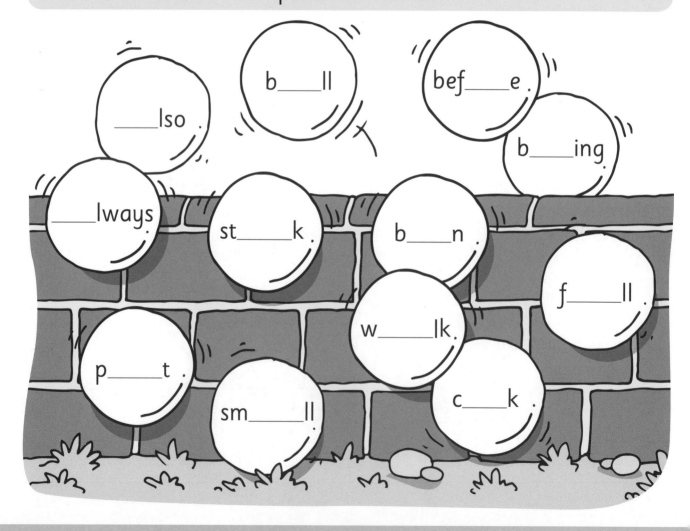

b____ll

bef____e

____lso

b____ing

____lways

st____k

b____n

f____ll

p____t

w____lk

sm____ll

c____k

How did you do?

War, wart, dwarf memory game

Read the words in the box and try to remember how to spell them.

> war   wart   warn   warm   dwarf
>
> swarm   towards   reward

There are some words where the /**or**/ sound after **w** is spelled **ar**. There are not very many, so try to learn them all.

Cover the words in the box above. Try to remember them all and write them in the spaces below.

w ___ ___

w ___ ___ ___

w ___ ___ ___

w ___ ___ ___

d ___ ___ ___ ___

s ___ ___ ___ ___

t ___ ___ ___ ___ ___ ___

r ___ ___ ___ ___ ___

Underline the word in each sentence that has the /**or**/ sound spelled **ar**.

1.   My mother has a wart at the end of her nose.

2.   Tilly was given a reward for having the best handwriting.

3.   It was lovely and warm by the fire.

4.   The dwarf sat on a blanket and read a book.

How did you do?

Fifteen-point challenge

Write labels for each of the pictures below.
Give yourself a point for each one you get right.

ch _ _ _ _ _

s _ _ _

d _ _ _ _

k _ _ _

s _ _ _

l _ _ _ _

w _ _ _ _

b _ _ _ _

f _ _ _

m _ _ _ _ _ _

g _ _ _ _ _ _

h _ _ _ _ _ _

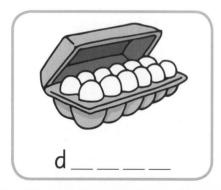
d _ _ _ _ _ _

b _ _ _ _ _ _ _

m _ _ _ _ _ _ _ _

How did you do?

Wa says wo

Circle the words in the wasps that make the /o/ sound and write them in the swan. One has been done for you.

When an /o/ sound follows a **w** it is often written **a**.

watch

Wash, want, swaps

Write the missing words to complete these sentences.

All the missing words have the letters **wa** that make the sound **wo**.

1. Sadly, Meera w_____ crying at school today.

2. Theo does not w_____ to do his homework.

3. Yesterday, we w_____ the school play in the hall.

4. Please can I sw_____ places with you?

5. "Keep close and don't w_____ off!" said Mrs Marek.

6. A sw_____ is another word for a bog or marsh.

7. It is polite to sw_____ your food before you speak.

8. Please w_____ your hands and come and sit down.

Write a sentence for these words.

swan _____

_____

watch _____

_____

How did you do?

Wor says wur

Write the words with the /**ur**/ sound in the circle. Cross out the words that do not have the /**ur**/ sound.

When an /**ur**/ sound follows a **w** it is often written **or**.

worse

word

worm

wor says **wur**

worship

worn

worry

sword

worth

work

Write the correct /**ur**/ words in the spaces below.

1. The bird ate a wriggly w_____.

2. Digging the garden is hard w_____.

3. Mrs Green gave us a really hard w_____ to spell.

4. I felt ill on Monday and even w_____ on Tuesday.

How did you do?

Want and worry practice

Read these words aloud.

Focus on the sounds made by the different letter patterns.

| wasp | what | wallet | watch | swan | swat |
| word | work | worth | worship | worm | worse |

What sound does the letter **a** make in these words?

_____

What sound do the letters **or** make in these words?

_____

Find all the words in the word search and circle them.

w	o	r	k	i	j	p	a	w	k
a	w	k	a	q	u	d	k	a	h
l	g	w	w	l	j	w	l	s	d
l	j	w	o	r	s	h	i	p	w
e	h	q	r	a	w	a	e	m	a
t	i	p	m	x	a	t	w	b	m
a	n	j	z	b	t	s	o	d	w
b	h	s	m	l	l	j	r	k	o
j	o	w	a	t	c	h	s	s	r
o	p	a	a	q	h	z	e	a	d
w	h	n	d	d	m	n	e	h	k
w	o	r	t	h	e	i	h	j	a

How did you do?

Changing y to i

When we add **es** to the end of words ending with **y**, we change the **y** into an **i** first. This is sometimes used to make plural nouns. (A noun can be a person, a place, a feeling, an object or an idea.)

Example: *one cherry, two cherries*:

cherry → cherri + es → cherries

Mohammed's multiplying machine makes plural words. Write the plurals for the words below.

fly	flies
cherry	
baby	
teddy	
pony	
party	
family	
bunny	
lady	

I fly, he flies

Sometimes we need to add **es** to the end of verbs (doing words) ending with **y**. To do this, we change the **y** into an **i** first.

Example: *I hurry*, *he hurries*: hurry → hurri + es → hurries

Write the missing words in the spaces.

I fly high.	The bird _flies_ high.
They fry mushrooms.	Sue _____ mushrooms.
I spy Mum.	Jon _____ Mum.
They dry quickly.	It _____ quickly.
I reply at once.	Meg _____ at once.
They magnify it.	It _____ them.
I multiply 5 x 5.	Jack _____ 5 x 5.
They tidy up.	Daisy _____ up.
I carry everything.	Mum _____ everything.
They hurry home.	Everyone _____ home.

How did you do?

I study, I studied

Fill in the missing words to change this diary entry into the past tense.

When we add **ed** to the end of verbs ending with **y**, we change the **y** into an **i** first.

copy → copied

Dear Diary

Today is not a good day. I try very hard at school but Mr Jones says I copy the answers from Jack. I deny it. After school I hurry home but I stop at the shop to buy eggs for Mum. Outside the shop is a little dog. I pity it being tied up. I carry the eggs home. At home I fry myself an egg but I burn the pan. I study in my room until Mum stops being cross.

Dear Diary

Today was not a good day. I _____ very hard at school but Mr Jones said I _____ the answers from Jack. I _____ it. After school I _____ home but I stopped at the shop to buy eggs for Mum. Outside the shop was a little dog. I _____ it being tied up. I _____ the eggs home. At home I _____ myself an egg but I burned the pan. I _____ in my room until Mum stopped being cross.

How did you do?

39

Hurry, hurrying

When we add **ing** to the end of verbs ending with **y**, we just add the ending.

copy → copy + ing → copying

Add **ing** to the end of these words.
Then use the new words to complete the sentences below.

deny →

carry →

reply →

copy →

bully →

worry →

1. The girls put up their anti-_____ poster.

2. "What are you _____ about?" asked Mum.

3. It's no good _____ it – I saw you do it!

4. I was in the middle of _____ to Granny's letter, when another arrived.

5. When you have finished _____ the list of words, you can go.

6. Uncle Josef arrived, _____ lots of parcels.

How did you do?

Early, earlier, earliest

When we add **er** and **est** to the end of adjectives (describing words) ending with **y**, we change the **y** into an **i** first.

lucky → luckier → luckiest

Add **er** and **est** to the end of these words.

early	earlier	earliest
heavy		
lovely		
curly		
angry		
bumpy		
tiny		
shiny		
icy		

How did you do?

Hike, hiking, hiked

Add **ed** and **ing** to the end of these words. Write the new words in the circles.

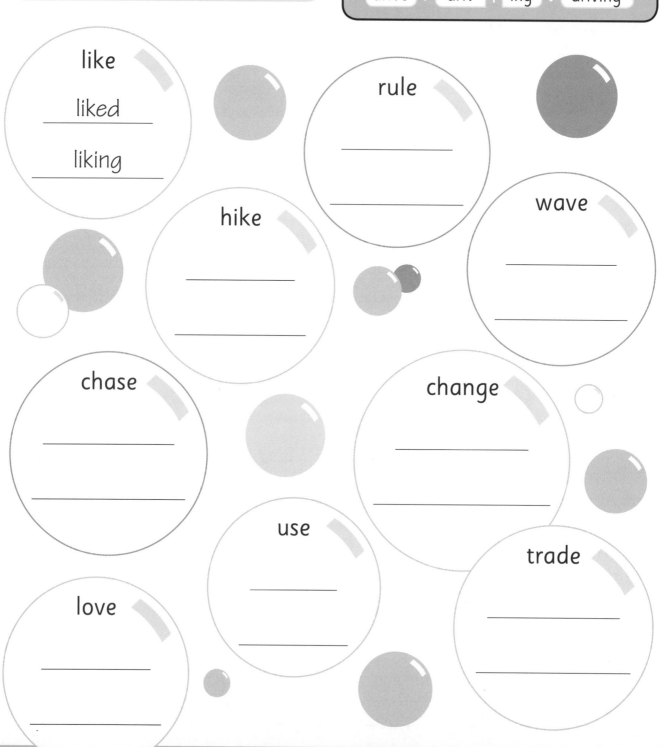

like
liked
liking

rule
_____
_____

wave
_____
_____

hike
_____
_____

chase
_____
_____

change
_____
_____

use
_____
_____

trade
_____
_____

love
_____
_____

How did you do?

A hiker and a biker

Complete these sentences.

When we add **er** and **est** to the end of words that end in **e**, we drop the **e** first.

| nice | → | nic | + | er | → | nicer |

| nic | → | nic | + | est | → | nicest |

1. The shops are close, but the school is <u>closer</u> and the park is <u>closest</u>.

2. A sheep is large, but a horse is _____ and an elephant is the _____.

3. Mr Jones is wise, but Mr Smith is _____ and Mrs Ward is the _____.

4. The bird is cute, but the cat is _____ and the dog is the _____.

Add er to these verbs to name who is doing them.

Word endings are sometimes called suffixes. The **er** and **est** suffixes can be used to compare things or to make names for people who do things.

5. I like to hike. I am a <u>hiker</u>.

6. I tame lions. I am a lion _____.

7. I explore the world. I am an _____.

8. Mrs Chen liked to write books. She was a _____.

9. I always share my toys. Mum says I am a good _____.

How did you do?

Spicy and bubbly

If we add a **y** to the end of a noun we create a describing word (an adjective). If the original word ends in an **e** we must take off the **e** before adding **y**.

stone → ston + y → stony

Create adjectives from these phrases.

full of juice	→	juicy
full of spice	→	
likes to cuddle	→	
covered in ice	→	
covered in grease	→	
lots of bounce	→	
like a mouse	→	
making lots of noise	→	

How did you do?

Past and present

When we add **ing** and **ed** to the end of these verbs, we double the last letter.

swim → swimming   slip → slipping   tap → tapped

These words all have one syllable (beat) and end in a single consonant.

There are 5 vowels in the English alphabet: **a**, **e**, **i**, **o**, **u**. All the other letters are consonants.

swim   slip   tap

Change the verbs below into the past tense by adding **ed**. Add **ing** to bring them back to the present.

hop   hopped

chat

drag

slip

grin

beg

hug

plug

How did you do?

Making objects crossword

Solve the clues to make objects to fill in the crossword.

You will need to double the last letter before adding **er**.

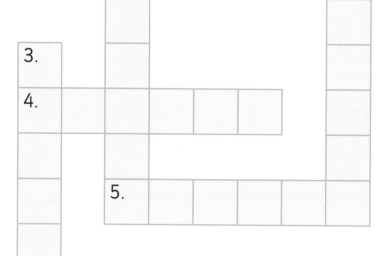

Down

1. flip + er

2. stop + er

3. shred + er

7. rap + er

Across

4. hop + er

5. rub + er

6. drop + er

8. slip + er

9. scan + er

How did you do?

Knotty and dotty

Add **y** to these nouns to make adjectives.

You will need to double the last letter.

dot
_____

knot
_____

snot
_____

fog
_____

fur
_____

sun
_____

Turn these adjectives back into nouns.

funny
_____

gappy
_____

You will need to remove the **y** and the doubled letter.

How did you do?

Literacy sum time

Check if you remember all the spelling rules from this chapter by solving these literacy sums.

1. ferry + es =

2. reply + es =

3. marry + ed =

4. carry + ing =

5. lucky + er =

6. dirty + est =

7. skate + ed =

8. decide + ing =

9. drive + er =

10. bubble + y =

11. run + y =

12. shop + ed =

How did you do?

Adding ment

Add **ment** to the end of these words.

retire_____   amaze_____   agree_____

move_____   pay_____   assess_____

Use the new words to complete these sentences

1. The children had an _____ in the afternoon.

2. We were filled with _____ when we saw our new kitten.

3. Josh and Jai were in _____ about the rules.

4. The _____ in the hedge was a blackbird.

5. Please give me your _____ for the school trip.

6. Grandpa looked forward to lots of gardening in his _____.

Split these words into their root word and ending.

appointment = _____ + _____

punishment = _____ + _____

How did you do?

Adding ness

If a word ends in a **y**, change the **y** to an **i** before adding the **ness** suffix.

Add **ness** to the end of these words. Write the new words on the lines.

sad _____

silly _____

dark _____

thick _____

happy _____

ill _____

Write each of the new words under the picture it matches.

_____

_____

_____

_____

_____

_____

How did you do?

Adding ly

Complete these word sums to fill in the crossword.

If a word ends with a **y**, change the **y** into an **i** before adding **ly**.

Across

3. like + ly

4. happy + ly

7. lucky + ly

10. easy + ly

11. bad + ly

Down

1. busy + ly

2. grumpy + ly

5. angry + ly

6. sudden + ly

8. crafty + ly

9. love + ly

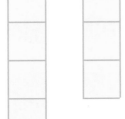

Adding ful

Add the **ful** suffix to each of the words in the mixing bowl. Write the new words in the bowl underneath.

Watch out for the words ending in **y**.

beauty   care   bowl
bag   arm   bucket
bash   duty

How did you do?

Fearless Jack

Add **less** to the end of these words.
Write the new words on the lines.

Watch out for words ending in **y**.

fear _____

count _____

penny _____

price _____

point _____

hope _____

Use each new word once to complete the sentences.

Every night a dragon burned the fields. Growing anything was _pointless_. Many knights went to fight the dragon but they were all _____ at fighting. "That's the last of the money, Jack," said his mother. "We are now completely _____." The princess said she would give a _____ jewel to the brave dragon slayer. Jack said he would go. He was not afraid of the dragon, in fact he was not afraid of anything – he was completely _____. Jack walked on and on for days and days. There were robbers, wolves and _____ other dangers along the road.

How did you do?

Choosing ment or ness

Add **ment** and **ness** to each word and fill in the table. Cross out the words that you think are not real.

> Reading the words aloud might help you to work out if they are real or not.

	ment	ness
pave	pavement	~~paveness~~
nervous		
employ		
mad		
sick		
commit		
settle		
willing		
treat		
hard		

Add **ment** or **ness** to these words.

apart _____

dark _____

ill _____

enjoy _____

How did you do?

Adding ful or less

Try adding **ful** and **less** to these words. If you think you have made a real word write it on the correct side.

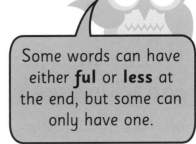

Some words can have either **ful** or **less** at the end, but some can only have one.

ful		less
useful	use	useless
	care	
	peace	
	power	
	hope	
	spot	
	harm	
	grate	
	tooth	
	help	
	pain	
	name	
	taste	

How did you do?

Adjective to noun

Write these words in the correct jam jar.

An adjective is a describing word. A noun is a person, a feeling, an animal, an object or an idea.

merry   payment   ill   ~~treatment~~   illness   ~~silly~~
merriment   silliness   treat   kindness   pay   kind

adjectives

silly

nouns

treatment

Complete these sentences using the words in the box below.

When we add **ment** to an _____ we create a _____.

When we add **ness** to an _____ we create a _____.

How did you do?

Noun to adjective

Write these words in the correct sack.

goal   thought   beautiful   ~~cheerful~~   home
goalless   dreadful   dread   homeless   help
thoughtless   painless   ~~pain~~   beauty   cheer   helpful

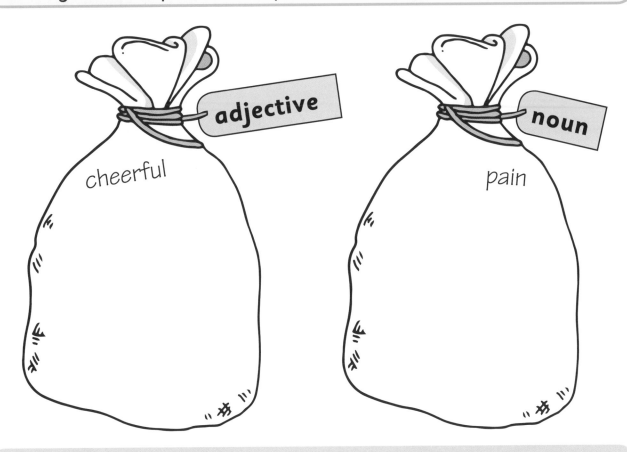

adjective

cheerful

noun

pain

Complete these sentences using the words in the box below.

When we add **ful**

to a _____ we create

an _____.

When we add **less**

to a _____ we create

an _____.

How did you do?

Adjective to adverb

Write these words in the correct bucket.

shy   cheerfully   neat   funnily
cheerful   carefully   fiercely   ~~sadly~~
~~funny~~   careful   slowly   fierce   neatly
shyly   sad   slow

An adjective is a word that describes a noun. An adverb is a word that describes how something is done.

adjective

funny

adverb

sadly

Complete this sentences using the words in the box.

adverb
adjective

When we add **ly** to an _____
we create an _____.

How did you do?

Come here so I can hear you

Circle the correct homophones to complete the sentences.

Homophones are words that sound the same but mean different things.

Speak louder – I can't **hear** / **here** you.

Hear / **Here** you are at last!

The **quiet** / **quite** mouse hid from the cat.

Mum thought her cake was **quiet** / **quite** good.

It is lovely to swim in the **see** / **sea** on holiday.

Cats and foxes can **see** / **sea** in the dark.

You should not go outside with **bear** / **bare** feet.

I can't **bear** / **bare** it when I lose a game.

There is just **won** / **one** sweet left.

My sister and I raced to the shops and I **won** / **one**.

How did you do?

The night in the knight

Draw a line to match the sentence to the correct missing word.

1. My parents have one daughter and one _____.

son

2. I look cool in the _____ in my hat and shades.

blue

3. I am _____ old for a babysitter.

two

4. Please try to go _____ sleep.

sun

5. There are _____ sweets left – one for me and... another for me.

blew

6. Please _____ gentle with the baby rabbit.

be

7. Ow! That _____ stung me.

to

8. I _____ out all the candles on my cake in one go.

too

9. Our school uniform is grey trousers and a _____ jumper.

bee

How did you do?

No, I don't know

Choose the correct homophone for each definition.

Homophones are words that sound the same but mean different things.

night knight

bye by

no know

paw poor

new knew

tale tail

they're there their

flour flower

1. A white powder used in making cakes. _____

2. A word you say when you are leaving. _____

3. The foot of a furry animal. _____

4. The opposite of yes. _____

5. Just bought from a shop. _____

6. The opposite of day. _____

7. The opposite of here. _____

8. A medieval soldier. _____

9. A dog wags it. _____

How did you do?

Spelling match

Find these tricky words in the sentences and underline them.

You could learn these sentences to help you remember how to spell the tricky words.

floor   poor   door   find   kind   mind   behind   old
cold   gold   hold   told   great   break   steak   would
could   should   move   prove   improve

1. Poor Cinderella had to wash the floor and the door.

2. If you mind your head, you can find the kind man behind the low door.

3. The old miner told us that he got hold of the gold in the cold river.

4. Jilly had a great big steak on her lunch break.

5. I should think you could do it if you would only try.

6. I will prove that you can improve your dance move.

How did you do?

Silly spelling

Underline the part of each word that makes it tricky to spell. Practise spelling the words using look, say, cover, write, check.

Look at the word.
Say the word aloud.
Cover the word.
Write the word.
Check the spelling of the word you have written.

	First attempt	Second attempt
sure		
sugar		
busy		
eye		
people		
because		
pretty		
wild		
climb		
most		
only		
many		

How did you do?

A long /ar/

Do you say these words with a short /**a**/ sound or a long /**ar**/ sound?

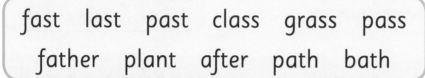

fast   last   past   class   grass   pass
father   plant   after   path   bath

Make up silly sentences using the words to help you remember them.

Words such as *fast*, *last* and *past* can be said with a short /**a**/ sound or a long /**ar**/ sound. If you say them with a long /**ar**/ sound, then you need to remember that the /**ar**/ sound is spelled **a**.

(fast, last, past)

The fast car has zoomed past us and now we're last.

(class, grass, pass) _____

_____

(father, plant) _____

_____

(after, path, bath) _____

_____

How did you do?

Tricky word search

Find these tricky words in the word search and circle them.

> every   even   everybody   beautiful   hour   who
> whole   any   clothes   again

e	v	e	r	y	b	o	d	y	c	k
v	f	g	j	a	u	d	z	l	l	l
e	w	m	s	a	j	w	w	h	o	e
n	o	a	y	u	w	c	b	a	t	s
t	w	a	g	v	q	k	p	h	h	u
i	h	e	v	e	r	y	l	s	e	b
b	o	d	g	k	a	j	e	s	s	z
a	l	g	a	g	a	i	n	b	h	c
m	e	s	a	g	h	a	i	c	o	a
d	a	b	e	a	u	t	i	f	u	l
o	e	h	r	n	a	g	h	k	r	u
w	a	k	f	y	q	a	a	j	z	o

How did you do?

Different types of sentences

Practise writing sentences using the pictures to get ideas.

Check your sentences using the checklist on page 68.

Write a question.

_____

_____

Write a sentence that ends with an exclamation mark.

_____

_____

Write a sentence with a comma.

_____

_____

Write a sentence that is a command.

_____

_____

How did you do?

Using tricky words

Write sentences using the tricky words below. Write each sentence in the past tense.

Check your sentences using the checklist on page 68.

1. _____

_____

_____

Christmas

2. _____

_____

_____

Mr, Mrs

3. _____

_____

_____

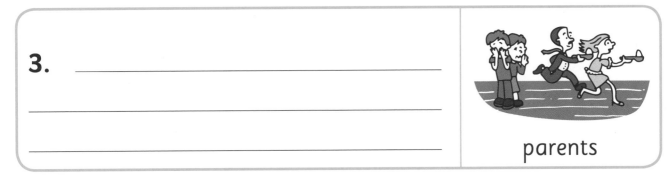
parents

4. _____

_____

_____

half, water

How did you do?

Using homophones

Write sentences using
the homophones below.
Try to make one a question.

Try to make your sentences as silly
as possible. The sillier they are,
the easier they will be to remember.

1. would, wood ___I would not like to live in a dark wood.___

2. sure, shore _____

3. I, eye _____

4. deer, dear _____

5. for, four _____

6. hole, whole _____

7. knot, not _____

Check your sentences using this checklist.

	I have started each sentence with a capital letter.
	I have finished each sentence with either a full stop, a question mark or an exclamation mark.
	I have checked my spelling.
	I have checked that my sentences make sense, even if they're silly!

How did you do?

Practising short versions

Write the short versions of these phrases.

Sometimes apostrophes are used to show that letters have been missed out in shortened versions of phrases.

Example: | I am → I'm |

| I am _____ | I will _____ |

| you are _____ | you will _____ |

| he is _____ | he will _____ |

| she is _____ | she will _____ |

| it is _____ | it will _____ |

| we are _____ | we will _____ |

| you are _____ | who will _____ |

| they are _____ | they will _____ |

Write a sentence using one of the new words above.

_____

_____

How did you do?

Don't, won't, can't

Write the short form of these phrases.

Sometimes apostrophes are used to show that letters have been missed out in shortened versions of phrases.

Example: | I am | ➜ | I'm |

could not _____

would not _____

should not _____

will not _____

might not _____

do not _____

cannot _____

shall not _____

had not _____

has not _____

have not _____

I have _____

you have _____

he has _____

she has _____

it has _____

Write a sentence using one of the new words above.

_____

_____

How did you do?

Shorten it

Use contractions to make these sentences shorter.

1. They have not got their swimming costumes.

_____

2. What is that noise?

_____

3. I would not do that if I were you!

_____

4. You must not jump on the bed.

_____

5. The horse cannot jump fences.

_____

6. I will bring the cake.

_____

7. They have been away for a long time.

_____

How did you do?

Lost property sort out

All these items have been found in lost property. Use the teacher's list to write a label for each one. Remember to use an apostrophe.

As well as being used in shortened words, apostrophes can be used to show possession. Example:

| the bag belongs to John → | John's bag |

Missing items
Mrs Chapman's class

John – bag

Tilly – hairband

Sophie – hat

Luke – jumper

Ben – shoes

Jack – shorts

Mia – recorder

Lily – book

How did you do?

Make it right

Read the signs in this picture. Underline the words that are missing apostrophes. Add the apostrophes in the correct places.

How did you do?

Which sort of s?

Which of these words need an apostrophe? Circle the correct spelling to complete the sentence.

A plural doesn't need an apostrophe.

I am going to **Grannys** / **Granny's** house after school today.

The **flowers** / **flower's** were covered in bees.

Please don't tread on the **dogs** / **dog's** tail.

I don't want **Hollys** / **Holly's** sister to come with us.

Tamsins / **Tamsin's** jumper has a hole in the elbow.

The **girls** / **girl's** could not stop giggling.

The frog sat at the **waters** / **water's** edge.

The **dancers** / **dancer's** wore pink tutus.

This **weeks** / **week's** spellings are on the board.

The **books** / **book's** ending was surprising.

Fridays / **Friday's** lunch was roast chicken.

Toucans / **Toucan's** have very large beaks.

How did you do?

Missing apostrophes

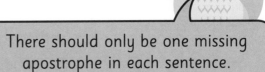

Add the missing apostrophe in each of these sentences.

There should only be one missing apostrophe in each sentence.

Its a beautiful day to take the dog for its walk.

Susies cats have been missing since Monday.

Dont leave your dirty socks on the sofa.

The boys have hidden the girls hat.

The farmers cows have escaped from the field.

Unfortunately the boy couldnt swim.

Jamies coming over to play today.

Orangutans live in the rainforests canopy.

If you tidy up the toys Ill buy you an ice cream.

Shell be coming round the mountain soon.

Auntie Mayas dogs are completely crazy.

Soon, polar bears wont have anywhere to live.

How did you do?

Get writing

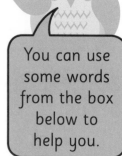

Write a caption for each of these pictures.
Use a word with an apostrophe in each caption.

You can use some words from the box below to help you.

don't   it's   I've   we're   they're   he's   Toby's

1. <u>Let's be quiet so we</u>

<u>don't wake the baby.</u>

2. _____

_____

3. _____

_____

4. _____

_____

How did you do?

A series of fortunate events

Write a caption for each of these pairs of pictures. Use a word with an apostrophe in each caption. Use **but** or **because** to extend your sentence.

You can use some words from the boxes to help you (but you don't have to).

---

didn't   wasn't   Sebastian   shoe   lace   caught

---

aren't   hadn't   couldn't

Use the checklist on page 68 to check your sentences.

How did you do?

Planes, trains and automobiles

Write a sentence about each of these pictures.

In each sentence include:

• a word with an apostrophe

• an adjective.

1. _____

_____

_____

2. _____

_____

_____

3. _____

_____

_____

4. _____

_____

_____

How did you do?

Animal watch

Write sentences to compare these animals.
For each sentence:
- use a word with an apostrophe
- write in the present tense
- connect ideas using **but** or **and**.

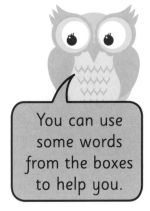

You can use some words from the boxes to help you.

1. _____

_____

_____

_____

monkey   tail   ape   doesn't

2. _____

_____

_____

_____

male   mane   female   hasn't

How did you do?

Well done!

Cut-out your reward Ollie.

Name:

....

You have completed

Spelling and vocabulary

For ages 6–7

Age: ....

Date: ....